A World Tour of Cultures

by Sharon Franklin

PEARSON

Scott
Foresman

Editorial Offices: Glenview, Illinois • Parsippany, New Jersey • New York, New York
Sales Offices: Needham, Massachusetts • Duluth, Georgia • Glenview, Illinois
Coppell, Texas • Ontario, California • Mesa, Arizona

Every effort has been made to secure permission and provide appropriate credit for photographic material. The publisher deeply regrets any omission and pledges to correct errors called to its attention in subsequent editions.

Unless otherwise acknowledged, all photographs are the property of Scott Foresman, a division of Pearson Education.

Photo locators denoted as follows: Top (T), Center (C), Bottom (B), Left (L), Right (R), Background (Bkgd)

Cover (C) ©Japack Company/Corbis, Cover (L) ©Bryan F. Peterson/Corbis, Cover (R) ©Michael S. Yamashita/Corbis; 1 ©Leonard de Selva/Corbis; 3 ©Dave Bartruff/Corbis; 4 ©Anthony Bannister; Gallo Images/Corbis; 5 (T) ©Bryan F. Peterson/Corbis, 6 (TL) ©Michael S. Yamashita/Corbis, 6 (TR) ©Jon Spaull/Corbis, 6 (B) ©Vince Streano/Corbis; 7 ©Gavriel Jecan/Corbis; 8 ©Japack Company/Corbis; 9 (Bkgd) ©Seattle Art Museum/ Corbis, 9 (C) ©Richard T. Nowitz/Corbis; 10 ©Leonard de Selva/Corbis; 11 ©Owen Franken/Corbis; 12 ©SETBOUN/Corbis; 13 ©Reza; Webistan/Corbis; 14 ©Jonathan Blair/ Corbis; 15 (B) ©Peter Johnson/Corbis, 15 (CL) ©Owen Franken/Corbis

ISBN: 0-328-13433-3

6 7 8 9 10 V0G1 14 13 12 11 10 09 08 07

This family is celebrating Chinese New Year. Sharing traditions helps tie families together.

The Call of Culture

What ties people together even when they are far apart? The answer is culture—the traditions and practices that people share. Culture includes language, food, songs, art, and clothing.

Let's visit Africa, Asia, and Europe. Can you find these continents in an **atlas**? Let's pack our bags and begin this cultural journey.

Talk and Culture

Language is a **vehicle** people use to pass down stories and traditions. In some cultures there is an oral tradition. A storyteller rises to tell and act out one of the old stories and then **reseats** himself or herself in the group. In this way, stories and songs are passed from one generation to another.

Africa has more than eight hundred languages. They all started from a single language. Some have died out because there is no one left who is **capable** of reading or writing them.

Bush people listen to a story, an important part of their culture and learning.

King Ludwig's castle, Neuschwanstein.

Home, Sweet Home

We can tell a lot about a people by their homes. The earliest people in Europe probably lived in caves. Wealthy kings and queens often lived in castles.

Today, most people live in apartments or houses. In the crowded European city of Amsterdam, though, people also live **aboard** houseboats along the canals.

Houses on stilts   A yurt

From Stilts to Junks to Yurts

Some houses in the Asian countries of Laos, Thailand, and Indonesia are perched on high, **awkward**-looking poles called stilts. These protect the houses from floods. In the crowded Hong Kong region of China, many families live on sturdy boats called junks.

Some people in Mongolia, in east-central Asia, don't live in one place. They travel with their cattle and carry their round tent houses—called yurts—with them.

A Hong Kong houseboat

Herds of cattle are led in and out
of a Masai village in Kenya.

Brothers for Life

The Masai people of Africa make their homes
in village communities in Kenya, in east Africa. As
many as five related families live in one house.
The boys from these families are grouped by age.
Their close relationship is like that of brothers.
They remain part of this group for life.

A Japanese woman wearing a kimono

What Are You Wearing, and Why?

Traditional clothing is another way that people keep their cultures alive.

In Scotland, tartans, or plaids, show a person's rank. A clan, or family, adopts its own special plaid. The more colors in the cloth, some say, the higher the position.

In the past, everyone in Japan wore kimonos. Kimonos are long gowns with wide sleeves. The wealthier you were, the more beautiful your kimono. Even today, handmade kimonos are worn for special occasions.

A Masai guide wearing beaded necklaces

The Culture of Colors

African countries are known for their brightly colored fabrics. Ghana is famous for its hand-woven *kente* cloth. The patterns in Masai beadwork let people know whether a woman is married or unmarried.

The colors used in traditional African clothing often have special meanings. For example, some Masai say the color green stands for peace.

Say It with Paper!

Paper was invented in China about A.D. 105. At first, it was made from bamboo, hemp, or mulberry plants. Only the rich could afford it. It took another 800 years before all Chinese could afford paper.

Paper is an important part of Chinese culture. During the spring New Year Festival in central China, people hang red paper cuttings to decorate their homes. This is thought to bring good luck.

The traditional art of Chinese papercutting takes years to master.

A candlemaker hangs a rack of hand-dipped candles to dry in his workshop in France.

The Beauty of Art

Art can capture our imaginations in many ways. A pyramid in Egypt looks like a **miracle**. Objects in a museum can show us how life was lived thousands of years ago.

Not all art is made to last through the ages. This candlemaker's amazing wax creations will soon burn away.

A Sami shaman holding
a ceremonial drum

Magic Drums

Lapland is an area north of the Arctic Circle
that includes part of Norway, Sweden, Finland,
and Russia. For nine months of every year, the
area is frozen and white with snow. But the Sami
of Lapland paint the sun on their drums!

Historically, Sami drums were not just used
to provide a **mechanical** rhythm. They played a
spiritual part as well. Sami priests used drums
when they talked to spirits and **chanted** their
prayers.

Yugur people, a Muslim minority in China

Why would a bride tuck a lump of sugar into her glove during a Greek wedding? Answer: To have a sweet life!

Delicious Traditions

Every culture has its own food traditions. For example, a typical Korean food is *kimch'i*, a spicy cabbage dish. Kimch'i is served at every meal, along with rice.

Jewish families celebrate the holiday of Hanukkah with *latkes.* They are pancakes made from potatoes that are shredded and fried in oil. A *Braai* is the South African version of a barbecue. Braai is a popular and delicious tradition.

Our Mix of Cultures

Our cultural heritage is everywhere. It is found in our clothing. It is mixed into our food. It is communicated by our language.

When groups of people live close together, it is easier to keep traditions alive. Then a tradition can repeat itself, generation after generation.

By honoring the traditions of our ancestors, we can be a part of something that has lasted for many years. What cultural traditions might you pass on?

Frying potato pancakes

A breakfast of tomatoes and sausages cooks on a grill in South Africa.

Glossary

aboard *adv.* on a ship, plane, bus, etc.

atlas *n.* book of maps.

awkward *adj.* not graceful in shape; clumsy.

capable *adj.* skilled, competent.

chanted *v.* said over and over again.

mechanical *adj.* like a machine; automatic.

miracle *n.* wonder.

reseats *v.* sits back down again.

vehicle *n.* means by which something is communicated, shown, or done.